It Takes

You

To Make

You

JUWE MOSES M.

DEDICATION

I dedicate this book to God almighty who has always been
there for me.

To my mother Esther for sending me to school at the right
age and time.

To my pastor for his encouragement and prayers always.

To my wife, for loving me and my beautiful children
Felicity, Feyikemi and Brian.

To you , for always reading and learning something new
from me.

Danke schön, Xièxiè nǐ, thank you.

ACKNOWLEDGMENTS

I acknowledge my friends and family for their continued support in this literary journey.

WHAT YOU NEED TO KNOW OR MAY KNOW AND NOT DO.

It's just all about you to make you

General Facts about life:

Don't wait, but move on with life because remember, the world is moving so why wait you.

Life doesn't give you what you deserve you take what you deserve out of life.

Until you can manage time; you can't manage anything in life.

Don't ever trust people because they will fail you. Trust God, then you will see them hail you.

When you are right doing the right thing no one remembers, but when you are wrong; even if only for once, no one forgets.

In life always try to keep your friends nervous and your enemies guessing.........

No one achieves success with with too many friends because when you follow the crowd you will miss the crown.

Don't ever trust and work with people who talks too much because they will soon drag you down.

If you have a friend who says this can't be done, then he his only telling you that he is ready to remain the same all life long

If you give too many reasons and excuses for your failure in things, then you are a failure yourself because you have truly failed.

Nothing under the sun is impossible because the sun looks impossible, yet, it is possible.

If you leave what you have to do pending till the next day. A fifty more will come knocking at your door and if you keep procrastinating then it becomes a burden and unachievable. Make hay while the sunshine and stop procrastinating.

He who builds according to every man's advice would have a crooked house.

Other Quotes from Scholars

You just need to try these…

"There are two things' people want more than sex and money…recognition and praise." - **Mary Kay Ash**

"The fairest thing we can experience is the mysterious. It is the fundamental emotion which stands at the cradle of true art and true science." - **Albert Einstein**

"Try to be better than yourself." - **William Faulkner**

"A great deal more is known than has been proved." - **Richard Feynman**

"I have yet to find the man, however exalted his station, who did not do better work and put forth greater effort under a spirit of approval than under a spirit of criticism." - **Charles M. Schwab**

"The ultimate court of appeal is observation and experiment--not authority." - **Thomas H. Huxley**

"Ignorance is the soil in which belief in miracles grows." - **Robert G. Ingersoll**

"Happiness is the meaning and purpose of life, the whole aim and the end of human existence." - **Aristotle**

"Valor grows by daring, fear by holding back" - **Publius Syrus**

"If the result confirms the hypothesis, then you've made a measurement. If the result is contrary to the hypothesis, then you've made a discovery." - **Enrico Fermi**

"The reproaches against science for not having yet solved the problems of the universe are exaggerated in an unjust and malicious manner; it has truly not had time enough yet for these great achievements. Science is very young - a human activity which developed late." - **Sigmund Freud**

"For far more marvelous is the truth than any artists of the past imagined it. Why do the poets of the present not speak of it? What men are poets who can speak of Jupiter if he were a man, but if he is an immense spinning sphere of methane and ammonia must be silent?" - **Richard Feynman**

"Colors fade, temples crumble, empires fall, but wise words endure." - **Edward Thorndike**

"The actions of men are the best interpreters of their thought." - **John Locke**

"Errors using inadequate data are much less than those using no data at all." - **Charles Babbage**

What a fiasco!

Do you know that...?

Success breeds confidence. Failure breeds discouragement and lack of confidence.

"You do not lead by hitting people over the head-- that's assault, not leadership." - **Dwight D. Eisenhower**

"Make the best use of what is in your power, and take the rest as it happens." – **Epictetus**

"Looking forward to things is half the pleasure of them." - **Lucy Maud Montgomery**

"The biggest reward for a thing well done is to have done it." – **Voltaire**

"Man who say it cannot be done should not interrupt man doing it." - **Chinese Proverb**

"If one loves, one loves the whole person as he or she is, and not as one might wish them to be." - **Leo Tolstoy**

"It is the working man who is the happy man. It is the idle man who is the miserable man." - **Benjamin Franklin**

The happiness of your life depends upon the quality of your thoughts: therefore, guard accordingly, and take care that you entertain no notions unsuitable to virtue and reasonable nature. - **Marcus Aurelius**

Make measurable progress in reasonable time. - **Jim Rohn**

There are two kinds of people one can call

reasonable: those who serve God with all their heart because they know him, and those who seek him with all their heart because they do not know him. - **Blaise Pascal**

Reason has always existed, but not always in a reasonable form. - **Karl Marx**

Reasonable men adapt to the world around them; unreasonable men make the world adapt to them. The world is changed by unreasonable men. -**Edwin Louis Cole**

You can't climb up to the second floor without a ladder. When you set your aim too high and don't fulfill it, then your enthusiasm turns to bitterness. Try for a goal that's reasonable, and then gradually raise it. -**Emil Zatopek**

It is not reasonable that those who gamble with men's lives should not pay with their own. - **H. G. Wells**

I am afraid of not living more than I am afraid of living wrong. - **Kaci Diane**

The time will pass anyway, you can either spend it

creating the life you want or spend it living the life you don't want. The choice is yours. – **Juwe Moses**

The best things in life are free. The second best are very expensive.

If you don't make the time to work on creating the life you want, you're eventually going to be forced to spend a lot of time dealing with a life you don't want. - **Kevin Ngo**

It is your reaction to adversity, not the adversity itself, that determines how your life's story will develop. - **Dieter F. Uchtdorf**

It is your reaction to adversity, not the adversity itself, that determines how your life's story will develop. - **Dieter F. Uchtdorf**

Life has no limitations; except the ones you make. - **Les Brown**

I Have Also Come To Realize That...

Sometimes the bad things that happen in our lives put us directly on the path to the best things that will ever happen to us.

Your attitude and the choices you make today will be your life tomorrow.

Life is the greatest journey you will ever be on.

Life is like a camera............ focus on what's important.. capture the good times. Develop from the negatives and if things don't work out TAKE ANOTHER SHOT.

Life is short. Break the rules forgive quickly, kiss slowly, love truly, laugh uncontrollably and never regret any thing that made you smile.

There's enough in this world for everybody's need. But not enough for certain people's good.

The 3c's of life: choices, chances, changes. You must make a choice to take a chance, or your life will never change.

Nobody in life gets exactly what they thought they were going to get. But if you work hard and you are kind, amazing things will happen. I'm telling you;

amazing things will happen.

If everyone is happy with you. Then surely you have made many compromises in your life. If you are happy with everyone. Surely you have ignored many faults of others.

Life is an opportunity. Benefit from it.

Life is beautiful. Admire it.

Life is a dream. Realize it.

Life is a challenge. Meet it.

Life is a duty. Complete it.

Life is a game. Play it.

Life is a promise. Fulfil it.

Life is a song. Sing it.

Life is an adventure. Dare it.

Life is life. Live for it.

Live as if you were to die tomorrow; learn as if you are to live forever.

If someone wants to be a part of your life they'll make an effort to be in it. Don't bother reserving a space in your heart for someone who doesn't make an effort to stay.

What lies behind you and what lies in front of you pales in comparison to what lies inside of you.

Never forget three 3 types of people in your life:

1. who helped you in your difficulty
2. who left you in your difficult time
3. who put you in difficult time

People are like oceans; some parts are invisible. But most you can't see shallow pools of truth and deep pools of dark mysteries.

Nobody can go back and start a new beginning, but anyone can start today and make a new ending.

Enjoy the little things in life for one day you'll look back and realize they were the big things.

Life is better when you are laughing.

Every story has an end. In life every ending is just a

new beginning.

You'll never be brave if you don't get hurt, you'll never learn if you don't make mistakes, and you'll never be successful if you don't encounter failure.

Never allow someone to be your priority while allowing yourself to be their option.

We all die in life. The goal isn't to live forever, the goal is to create something that will live forever.

We are all here for special reason. Stop being a prisoner of your past. Become the architect of your future.

Learn from yesterday, love for today, hope for tomorrow. The important thing is to not stop questioning.

Being honest may not get you a lot of friends but it'll always get you the right ones.

Life is like a coin you can spend it any way you wish but you only spend it once.

Success always hugs you in private.........! But

"failure always slaps you in the public….!" That's life.

In three words I can sum up everything I've learned about life. It goes on.

In life we do things. Some we wish we had never done. Some we wish we could replay a million times in our heads. But they all make us who we are and, in the end, they shape every details about us. If we were to reverse any of them, we wouldn't be the person we are. So just live life. Make mistakes. Have wonderful memories. But never ever second guess who you are, where you have been and most importantly where it is you are going.

Life is like riding a bike. It is important to maintain your balance while standing still.

People miss you more when they see how much happier you are in life without them.

It is a risk to love. What if it doesn't work out? Ah, but if it does... **Peter MC Williams**

In life every new year is another 12 months, 52 weeks, 365 days, 8,760 hours,525,600 minutes and 3,153,600 seconds of heart breaks, progress and new experience.

If you correct your mind, the rest of your life will fall into place.

Don't choose the one who is beautiful in the world. But rather, choose the one who makes your world beautiful.

Live life, laugh lot and love forever.

No matter how serious life gets, you still got to have that one person you can be completely stupid with.

Someday everything will all make perfect sense. So, for now, laugh at the confusion, smile through the tears, and keep reminding yourself that everything happens for a reason

Stop worrying about what you have to lose and start focusing on what you have to gain.

Life $+laughter*love-hate=happiness$. Live life and be happy.

Fall seven times, stand up eight.

God didn't promise days without pain, laughter without sorrow, sun without rain, but he did promise strength for the day, comfort for the tears and light for the way.

Action speaks louder than words. We can apologize over and over but if our actions don't change, the words become meaningless.

Never let your memories be greater than your dreams.

Life is just a phase you are going thru you will get over it.

Life always offer you a second chance. It is called tomorrow.

Life may not be the party we hoped for, but while we are here, we might as well dance.

Life is too short to worry, life is too long to wait.

The moment you are ready to quit is usually the moment right before the miracle happens.

If you want something you've never had, then you've got to do something you've never done.

Never blame anyone in your life. The good people give you happiness. The bad people give you experience. The worst people give you a lesson. The best people give you memories.

Sixty (60) Things You Need To Understand in Order To Live A Peaceful Life

1.   You cannot change what you refuse to confront.

2.   Sometimes good things fall apart so better things can fall together.

3.   Don't think of cost. Think of value.

4.   Sometimes you need to distance yourself to see things clearly.

5.   Too many people buy things they don't need with money they don't have to impress people they don't know. **Read- Rich Dad, Poor Dad.**

6.   No matter how many mistakes you make or how slow you progress, you are still way ahead of everyone who isn't trying.

7.   If a person wants to be a part of your life, they will make an obvious effort to do so. Think twice before reserving a space in your heart for people who do not make an effort to stay.

8.   Making one person smile can change the world – maybe not the whole world, but their world.

9.   Saying someone is ugly doesn't make you any prettier.

10.   The only normal people you know are the ones you don't know very well.

11.   Life is 10% of what happens to you and 90% of how you react to it.

12.   The most painful thing is losing yourself in the process of loving someone too much and forgetting that you are special too.

13.   It's better to be alone than to be in bad company.

14.   As we grow up, we realize it becomes less important to have more friends and more important

to have real ones.

15.   Making a hundred friends is not a miracle. The miracle is to make a single friend who will stand by your side even when hundreds are against you.

16.   Giving up doesn't always mean you're weak, sometimes it means you are strong enough and smart enough to let go and move on.

17.   Don't say you don't have enough time. You have exactly the same number of hours per day that were given to Helen Keller, Pasteur, Michelangelo, Mother Teresa, Leonardo da Vinci, Thomas Jefferson, Albert Einstein, etc…

18.   If you really want to do something, you'll find a way. If you don't, you'll find an excuse.

19.   Don't choose the one who is beautiful to the world; choose the one who makes your world beautiful.

20.   Falling in love is not a choice. To stay in love is.

21.   True love isn't about being inseparable; it's about two people being true to each other even when they are separated.

22.   While you're busy looking for the perfect person, you'll probably miss the imperfect person who could make you perfectly happy.

23.   Never do something permanently foolish just because you are temporarily upset.

24.   You can learn great things from your mistakes when you aren't busy denying them. **Read The 7 Habits of Highly Effective People.**

25.   In life, if you don't risk anything, you risk everything.

26.   When you stop chasing the wrong things you give the right things a chance to catch you.

27.   Everything that has ever happened in your life is preparing you for a moment that is yet to come.

28.   There isn't anything noble about being superior to another person. True nobility is in being

superior to the person you once were.

29.   Trying to be someone else is a waste of the person you are.

30.   You will never become who you want to be if you keep blaming everyone else for who you are now.

31.   People are more what they hide than what they show.

32.   Sometimes people don't notice the things others do for them until they stop doing them.

33.   Don't listen to what people say, watch what they do.

34.   Being alone does not mean you are lonely and being lonely does not mean you are alone.

35.   Love is not about sex, going on fancy dates, or showing off. It's about being with a person who makes you happy in a way nobody else can.

36.   Anyone can come into your life and say how much they love you. It takes someone really special to stay in your life and show how much they love you.

37.   Burn the candles, use the nice sheets, wear the fancy lingerie. Don't save it for a special occasion; today is special.

38.   Love and appreciate your parents. We are often so busy growing up, we forget they are also growing old.

39.   When you have to start compromising yourself and your morals for the people around you, it's probably time to change the people around you.

40.   Learn to love yourself first, instead of loving the idea of other people loving you.

41.   When someone tells you, "You've changed," it might simply be because you've stopped living your life their way.

42.   Someone else doesn't have to be wrong for you to be right.

43.   Be happy. Be yourself. If others don't like it, then let them be. Happiness is a choice. Life isn't about pleasing everybody.

44.   When you're up, your friends know who you are. When you're down, you know who your friends are.

45.   Don't look for someone who will solve all your problems; look for someone who will face them with you.

46.   If you expect the world to be fair with you because you are fair, you're fooling yourself. That's like expecting the lion not to eat you because you didn't eat him.

47.   No matter how good or bad you have it, wake up each day thankful for your life. Someone somewhere else is desperately fighting for theirs.

48.   The smallest act of kindness is worth more than the grandest intention.

49.   Many people are so poor because the only thing they have is money.

50.   Learn to appreciate the things you have before time forces you appreciate the things you once had.

51.   When you choose to see the good in others, you end up finding the good in yourself.

52.   You don't drown by falling in the water. You drown by staying there.

53.   It's better to know and be disappointed than to never know and always wonder.

54.   There are things that we don't want to happen but have to accept, things we don't want to know but have to learn, and people we can't live without but have to let go.

55.   Happiness is not determined by what's happening around you, but rather what's happening inside you. Most people depend on others to gain happiness, but the truth is, it always comes from within.

56.   If you tell the truth, it becomes a part of your past. If you lie, it becomes a part of your future.

57.   What you do every day matters more than what you do every once in a while. **Read The Power of Habit**.

58.   You can't start the next chapter of your life if you keep re-reading your last one.

59.   Things turn out best for people who make the best out of the way things turn out.

60.   If you don't like something, change it. If you can't change it, change the way you think about it.

Just know, when you truly want success, you'll never give up on it. No matter how bad the situation may get

"I don't regret the things I've done; I regret the things I didn't do when I had the chance

"Challenges are what make life interesting and overcoming them is what makes life meaningful

"It's hard to wait around for something you know might never happen; but it's harder to give up when you know its everything you want." – **Baron James**

"One of the most important keys to Success is having the discipline to do what you know you should do, even when you don't feel like doing it." – **Juwe**

Moses

"Good things come to those who wait… greater things come to those who get off their ass and do anything to make it happen." – **Could be you**

"Happiness cannot be traveled to, owned, earned, or worn. It is the spiritual experience of living every minute with love, grace & gratitude." - **Denis Waitley**

"In order to succeed, your desire for success should be greater than your fear of failure." – **Bill Cosby**

"Go where you are celebrated – not tolerated. If they can't see the real value of you, it's time for a new start." – **Could be you**

Don't be afraid to stand for what you believe in, even if that means standing alone.. – **Juwe Moses**

"The best revenge is massive success." – **Frank Sinatra**

"Forget all the reasons it won't work and believe the

one reason that it will." – **Juwe Moses**

"I am thankful for all of those who said NO to me. It's because of them I'm doing it myself." – **Albert Einstein**

"The only way to do great work is to love what you do. If you haven't found it yet, keep looking. Don't settle." – **Steve Jobs**

"Life is short, live it. Love is rare, grab it. Anger is bad, dump it. Fear is awful, face it. Memories are sweet, cherish it." – **Could be you**

"When you say "It's hard", it actually means "I'm not strong enough to fight for it". Stop saying its hard. Think positive!" - **Could be you**

"Life is like photography. You need the negatives to develop." - **Could be you**

"Don't worry about failures, worry about the chances you miss when you don't even try." – **Jack Canfield**

"The pain you feel today is the strength you feel tomorrow. For every challenge encountered there is opportunity for growth." - **Could be you**

"Build your own dreams, or someone else will hire you to build theirs." – **Farrah Gray**

"The only thing that stands between you and your dream is the will to try and the belief that it is actually possible." – **Joel Brown**

"Self-confidence is the most attractive quality a person can have. how can anyone see how awesome you are if you can't see it yourself?" – **C. JoyBell C.**

"We learn something from everyone who passes through our lives.. Some lessons are painful, some are painless.. but all are priceless." – **Brian Tracy**

"Being happy doesn't mean that everything is perfect. it means that you've decided to look beyond the imperfections." - Unknown

"Nobody ever wrote down a plan to be broke, fat, lazy, or stupid. Those things are what happen when you don't have a plan." – **Larry Winget**

"Three things you cannot recover in life: the WORD

after it's said, the MOMENT after it's missed and the TIME after it's gone. Be Careful!" – Unknown

"Though no one can go back and make a brand-new start, anyone can start from now and make a brand new ending." – **Carl Bard**

"When the past calls, let it go to voicemail, believe me, it has nothing new to say." - **Unknown**

"Rule #1 of life. Do what makes YOU happy." – **Juwe Moses**

"Walk away from anything or anyone who takes away from your joy. Life is too short to put up with fools." – **Unknown**

"Love what you have. Need what you want. Accept what you receive. Give what you can. Always remember, what goes around, comes around…" – **Unknown**

"Just remember there is someone out there that is more than happy with less than what you have." – **Unknown**

"The biggest failure you can have in life is making the mistake of never trying at all." – **Unknown**

"Life has two rules: #1 Never quit #2 Always remember rule # 1." - **Unknown**

"No one is going to hand me success. I must go out & get it myself. That's why I'm here. To dominate. To conquer. Both the world, and myself." - **Unknown**

Life isn't simple. But the beauty of it is, you can always start over. It'll get easier. **Alacia Bessette, Simply from Scratch, 2010**

Life is indeed difficult, partly because of the real difficulties we must overcome in order to survive, and partly because of our own innate desire to always do better, to overcome new challenges, to self-actualize. Happiness is experienced largely in striving towards a goal, not in having attained things, because our nature is always to want to go on to the next endeavor.

Albert Ellis, Michael Abrams, Lidia Dengelegi, The Art & Science of Rational Eating, 1992

There are two ways to slide easily through life: to believe everything or to doubt everything; both ways save us from thinking. - **Alfred Korzybski (1879 - 1950)**

You're alive. Do something. The directive in life, the moral imperative was so uncomplicated. It could be expressed in single words, not complete sentences. It sounded like this: Look. Listen. Choose. Act. - **Barbara Hall, A Summons to New Orleans, 2000**

The first step to getting the things you want out of life is this: Decide what you want. - **Ben Stein**

Man is born to live, not to prepare for life. - **Boris Pasternak (1890 - 1960), Doctor Zhivago, 1958**

Not a shred of evidence exists in favor of the idea that life is serious. - **Brendan Gill**

You don't have to live your life so that your life is suitable for small talk. Life can be lived in ways that circumnavigate a myriad of colors and landscapes. - **Cherie Ve Ard, Technomadia, 04-04-2013**

Life is a foreign language; all men mispronounce it. **-**

Christopher Morley (1890 - 1957)

Life is full of surprises and serendipity. Being open to unexpected turns in the road is an important part of success. If you try to plan every step, you may miss those wonderful twists and turns. Just find your next adventure-do it well, enjoy it-and then, not now, think about what comes next. - **Condoleeza Rice**

In matters of self-control as we shall see again and again, speed kills. But a little friction really can save lives. - **Daniel Akst, We Have Met the Enemy: Self-Control in an Age of Excess, 2011**

When we exercise self-control on a given occasion, we win for ourselves a little credibility we can rely on the next time around. Pretty soon we develop a reputation to ourselves that we want badly to uphold. With each test that we meet, our resolve gains momentum, fueled by the fear that we may succumb and establish a damaging precedent for our own weakness. **Daniel Akst, We Have Met the Enemy: Self-Control in an Age of Excess, 2011**

Life is a thing that mutates without warning, not

always in enviable ways. All part of the improbable adventure of being alive, of being a brainy biped with giant dreams on a crazy blue planet.

Diane Ackerman, One Hundred Names for Love: A Stroke, A Marriage, and the Language of Healing, 2011

The purpose of life is to fight maturity. - **Dick Werthimer**

Oh, life is a glorious cycle of song,

A medley of extemporanea;

And love is a thing that can never go wrong;

And I am **Marie of Romania. - Dorothy Parker (1893 - 1967), Not So Deep as a Well (1937), "Comment"**

It's not true that life is one damn thing after another; it is one damn thing over and over. - **Edna St. Vincent Millay (1892 - 1950)**

Life is just one damned thing after another. - **Elbert Hubbard (1856 - 1915)**

Life is like one big Mardi Gras. But instead of showing your boobs, show people your brain, and if they like what they'll, you'll have more beads than you know what to do with. - **Ellen DeGeneres, Tulane Commencement Speech, 2009**

Life is something that happens when you can't get to sleep. - **Fran Lebowitz**

Life is not a spectacle or feast; it is a predicament. - **George Santayana (1863 - 1952)**

Life is something that everyone should try at least once. -**Henry J. Tillman**

Life is pleasant. Death is peaceful. It's the transition that's troublesome. - **Isaac Asimov (1920 - 1992)**

Life is difficult and complicated and beyond anyone's total control, and the humility to know that will enable you to survive its vicissitudes. - **J. K. Rowling, Harvard Commencement Address, 2008**

Life is a long lesson in humility. - **James M. Barrie (1860 - 1937)**

He only earns his freedom and existence who daily conquers them anew. - **Johann Wolfgang von Goethe (1749 - 1832)**

Life is what happens to you while you're busy making other plans. - **John Lennon (1940 - 1980), "Beautiful Boy"**

In real life, however, you don't react to what someone did; you react only to what you think she did, and the gap between action and perception is bridged by the art of impression management. If life itself is but what you deem it, then why not focus your efforts on persuading others to believe that you are a virtuous and trustworthy cooperator? - **Jonathan Haidt, The Happiness Hypothesis: Finding Modern Truth in Ancient Wisdom, 2005**

The lessons this life has planted in my heart pertain more to caring than crops, more to Golden Rule than gold, more to the proper choice than to the popular choice. - **Kirby Larson, Hattie Big Sky, 2006**

Life isn't like books. Books got somebody writing then and trying' to entertain you. Life is more like a set of Legos. Unless you take care of them, you lose a few pieces and you end up stepping on them with bare feet. You've got to take care of your life. - **Laura Moncur (1969 -), Merriton: life. Home, 02-29-12 35 Minutes Away From Home, 02-29-12**

Never climb a fence for someone who cannot jump a gutter for you. - **Juwe Moses**

Never allow compassion to take away the passion of your vision. - **Juwe Moses**

Three things chase you every day: Destruction, Death, and Thieves. Do not allow destiny destroyers that could lead to your death steal away your destiny and vision for life. Run of them always. - **Babawale Aduroshakin**

you can only appreciate the ART of mercy when you fall into the HANDS that avenge offences. - **Babawale Aduroshakin**

Learn to defend people that you love and appreciate.

They are the ones to promote you. People that we love are those we can stand with in their darkest hour no matter what it takes. - **Babawale Aduroshakin**

The only thing that stands between a person and what they want in life is the will to try it and the faith to believe it is possible. - **Rich De Vos**

Stop searching the world for treasure, the real treasure is in yourself. - **Pablo**

Life is a bowl of cherries. Some cherries are rotten while others are good; it's your job to throw out the rotten ones and forget about them while you enjoy eating the ones that are good!

There are two kinds of people: those who choose to throw out the good cherries and wallow in all the rotten ones, and those who choose to throw out all the rotten ones and savour all the good ones. - **C. Joy Bell C.**

There is a magnificent, beautiful, wonderful painting in front of you! It is intricate, detailed, a painstaking labour of devotion and love! The colours are like no other, they swim and leap, they trickle and embellish! And yet you choose to fixate your eyes on the small fly which has landed on it! Why do you do such a thing? - **C.Joy Bell C.**

HOW YOUR ATTITUDE REACTS FOR; AND AGAINST YOU

A bad attitude is like a flat tire. If you don't change it, you are going nowhere.

Read what scholars said about it ...

Attitude is a little thing that makes a big difference.
Winston Churchill

Difference makes your attitude, not your aptitude, will determine your altitude.

Zig Ziglar

Develop an attitude of gratitude, and give thanks for everything that happens to you, knowing that every step forward is a step toward achieving something bigger and better than your current situation.

Brian Tracy

There is little difference in people, but that little difference makes a big difference. The little difference is attitude. The big difference is whether it is positive or negative.

W. Clement Stone

If you don't have time to do it right, when will you have time to do it over?

John wooden

No matter how many people believe or don't believe in you, you must be the ultimate believer in yourself!

Pablo

Choosing to be positive and having a grateful attitude is going to determine how you're going to live your life.

Joel Osteen

Weakness of attitude becomes weakness of character.

Albert Einstein

Nothing can stop the man with the right mental attitude from achieving his goal; nothing on earth can help the man with the wrong mental attitude.

Thomas Jefferson

Your living is determined not so much by what life brings to you as by the attitude you bring to life; not so much by what happens to you as by the way your mind looks at what happens.

Khalil Gibran

My attitude is that if you push me towards something that you think is a weakness, then I will turn that perceived weakness into a strength.

Michael Jordan

If you look the right way, you can see that the whole world is a garden.

Frances Hodgson Burnett

I do not believe in taking the right decision. I take a decision and make it right.

Muhammad Ali Jinnah

If you can quit, quit. If you can't quit, stop complaining – this is what you chose.

J.A. Konrath

What is the difference between an obstacle and an opportunity? Our attitudes toward it. Every opportunity has a difficulty, and every difficulty has an opportunity.

J. Sidlow Baxter

If you say you can or you can't, you are right either way.

Henry Ford

Our beliefs about what we are and what we can be precisely determine what we can be.

Anthony Robbins

A positive attitude is most easily arrived at through a deliberate and rational analysis of what's required to manifest unwavering positive thought patterns. First, reflect on the actual, present condition of your mind. In other words, is the mind positive or not? We have all met individuals who perceive themselves as positive people but don't appear as such. Since the mind is both invisible and intangible, it's therefore easier to see the accurate characteristics of the mind through a person's words, deeds and posture.

For example, if we say, "It's absolutely freezing today! I'll probably catch a cold before the end of the day!" then our word exposes a negative attitude. But if we say, "The temperature is very cold" (a simple statement of fact), then our expression and attitude are not negative.

Sustaining an alert state in which self-awareness becomes possible gives us a chance to discover the origins of negativity. In doing so, we also have an opportunity to arrive at a state of positiveness, so that our words and deeds are also positive, making others feel comfortable, cheerful, and inspired.

H.E Davey

If you are unclear about what attitudes you adhere to, you will have a difficult time evaluating which ones are not serving your highest good.

Deborah Day

No matter how bad things get, just keep looking up. Just keep looking up above and never for one minute look down

Juwe Moses

Cultivate an optimistic mind, use your imagination, always consider alternatives, and dare to believe that you can make possible what others think is impossible.

Rodolfo Costa

When you are joyful, when you say 'yes' to life and have fun and project positivity all around you, you become a sun in the center of every constellation, and people want to be near you.

Shannon L. Alder

A positive attitude may not solve all our problems but that is the only option we have if we want to get out of problems.

Subodh Gupta

Believing in negative thoughts is the single greatest obstruction to success.

Charles F. Glassman

Live your everyday extraordinary!

Charles F. Glassman

People submit too easily to change from others. And yet, for some reason, whenever they consider changing themselves, the focus is always on what they are giving up, never what they are about to gain.

Chris Murray

Everything you desire is always just outside your comfort zone, dear boy. If it wasn't you would already possess it. Would you not?

Chris Murray

Trust me. If you do not decide where you are heading, and refuse to take the appropriate action, you will end up being shaped into what others would have you become. Then any change will not be made for your benefit but for theirs.

Chris Murray

Keep your thoughts positive because your thoughts become your words. Keep your words positive because your words become your behaviour. Keep your behaviour positive because your behaviour becomes your habits. Keep your habits positive because your habits become your values. Keep your values positive because your values become your destiny.

Mahatma Gandhi

Don't waste your time with explanations: people only hear what they want to hear.

Paulo Coelho

It Takes You To Make You

We can complain because rose bushes have thorns, or rejoice because thorn bushes have roses

Abraham Lincoln

The greater part of our happiness or misery depends upon our dispositions, and not upon our circumstances.

Martha Washington

Our life is what our thoughts make it.

Marcus Aurelius

Ability is what you are capable of doing. Motivation determines what you do. Attitude determines how well you do it.

Lou Holtz

Everyday one should at least hear one little song, read one good poem, see one fine painting and – if at all possible – speak a few sensible words.

Johann Wolfgang Von Goethe

Reject your sense of injury and the injury itself

disappears.

Marcus Aurelius

Look on every exit as being an entrance somewhere else.

Tom Stoppard

If you think you are beaten, you are.

If you think you dare not, you don't.

If you would like to win, but think you can't, it's almost a cinch you won't.

If you think you will lose, you have lost, for out in the world we find success being with a fellow's will; it's all in the state of mind.

If you think you are outclassed, you are: You've got to think high to rise. You've got to be sure of yourself before you can ever win a prize.

Life's battles don't always go to the stronger or faster man, but soon or late, the man who wins is the one who thinks he can.

Walter D. Wintle

We cannot change our past ... we cannot change the fact that people will act in a certain way. We cannot change the inevitable. The only thing we can do is play on the one string we have, and that is our attitude.

I am convinced that life is 10% what happens to me and 90% of how I react to it. And so it is with you… we are in charge of our 'Attitudes'.

Charles R. Swindoll

I am still determined to be cheerful and happy, in whatever situation I may be; for I have also learned from experience that the greater part of our happiness or misery depends upon our dispositions, and not upon our circumstances.

Martha Washington

To know a man's library is, in some measure, to know a man's mind.

Geraldine Brooks